Homes That They Share

by Dawn Tanner, Nancy Leasman, and Jim Perry

Leatherwood Publishing
20395 County Road 86
Long Prairie, MN 56347

ISBN 0-9741725-4-5

Printed and bound by Sunray Printing, St. Cloud, MN.

This book is printed on recycled paper.

Introduction

Families come in all shapes, sizes, colors and combinations. Families in every state and country enjoy going to the zoo and sharing the wonders of the natural world. Zoos provide us with unique opportunities to spend time watching animals. We would have little chance of even catching a glimpse of many of these creatures in the wild. This book helps parents and children understand the value of animals in the wild, focusing especially on exciting and often endangered species that we can see in zoos. If we protect large animals that need a lot of space to survive, we also save an amazing variety of other, equally valuable plants and animals.

Imagine yourself and your family in each of these pages. Join the families from around the world shown here and spend a day at the zoo. Learn about animals and their homes in the wild. Zoos play an important role in conservation and in educating people about the value of wild animals and wild places. How are the experiences from your day at the zoo the same as or different from the ones you see pictured here? Each animal profiled in this book is associated with a wide range of other animals and plants in its native landscape. Many of these other species are also found in zoos. See how many of these animals you and your family can find as a way of extending your day at the zoo. Record your favorite memories by pressing pennies at your zoo and mounting them on the pages. A dab of super glue will hold each penny in place.

glue in this circle
mount penny here

At the zoo today, I saw animals peeking out of corners, hiding in caves and hanging from trees all around me. I saw their bright colors and sparkling eyes. Some animals had scruffy backs. Others had long, tangley hair. Some called to me with loud grunts and squeals. Sometimes they made no noise at all. I imagined what it would feel like to have a hairy coat, fly through the air or swing from branches. I wondered "Why do animals need wild places when we can visit them at the zoo?"

The jaguar gave me a sly glance and slipped into its pool. Its fur was sleek and inky black. When the sun hit its back just right, I could see delicate patterns on its skin under the fur.

A jaguar on the prowl searches for prey in dense forests and wetlands. Jaguars like to stick close to water where they even capture caiman and anaconda, other powerful predators that lurk in the water. Ancient Mayans and Aztecs revered the jaguar, but modern humans are using more and more jaguar habitat for growing crops. If we protect jaguars, we also protect agile spider monkeys, colorful macaws, reclusive tapir, eyelash vipers and giant anteaters that are found in the home that they share.

As I rounded a corner, I saw Asian wild horses galloping, shaking their heads and curling their lips back in a funny kind of smile that helps them smell. The fresh spring air tousled their black shining manes. Their coats were shimmering gold against the grass around them.

Asian wild horses are the only truly wild horse left in the world. These horses, called *takhi*, still can be found in the wild because people at zoos have worked with park managers to bring takhi back to the steppe lands. Takhi again run free, mate and raise their young in the wilderness. If we protect Asian wild horses, we also protect Mongolian gazelles, marmots, demoiselle cranes and rare plants that are found in the home that they share.

I watched the Mexican wolves racing through the cactus and brush in their zoo home. The sunlight glinted off their coats. How fierce they must look running among prickly cactus in the desert wilderness.

Wolves eat other animals. Ranchers hunted wolves for many years to keep wolves from eating livestock. Now there are only a few Mexican wolves left in the wild, but many people are working to bring wolves back to the desert southwest of the United States and northern Mexico. If we protect Mexican wolves, we also protect Gila monsters, golden eagles, ocelots and desert lupine that are found in the home that they share.

The grizzly bears were sleeping in the shade when I spotted them. They woke up, shook their heavy fur coats like my dog does at home and lumbered into the sunshine. They were so curious. One bear splashed into the water, playing with a stick until he crushed it into a bunch of floaty pieces.

Grizzly bears used to roam across much of Canada and the United States. These bears eat elk, mountain goats and rodents. They also like berries, roots, nuts, and they even catch moths. Grizzly bears need a lot of space. If we protect grizzly bears, we also protect alpine forests, river valleys, cutthroat trout and berry patches that are found in the home that they share.

A flash of white fur swooped through the trees and darted inside. I waited and wondered what it could be. A moment later, the white-handed gibbon was back with its mate. They looped through the branches together, their long arms swinging them swiftly through the trees.

Gibbons are our smallest apes. They spend their lives in the dense forest canopy of Southeast Asia. A young gibbon stays with mom and dad for five to six years before starting a family of its own. Fruits are found in small patches in these huge forests, and gibbons need many fruit trees to feed themselves and their babies. Male and female gibbons sing duets together to defend their territory. Their eerie hooting calls echo through the forest in the morning and evening, announcing a chorus of life. If we protect the forests for gibbons, we also protect secretive clouded leopards, orangutans, flamboyant hornbills, Asian elephants and the world's largest flower, the *Rafflesia*, that are found in the home that they share.

I gasped when I saw a Siberian tiger tackle a cardboard animal that had a piece of meat hidden inside. Enrichment activities like finding food are used to help zoo animals stay healthy and keep them from getting bored. Many zoos have special activities like this one. I was lucky to see one today.

Very few Siberian tigers are left in the world today. Tigers are killed because their bones, ground up in medicines, are used to treat human illnesses. Humans also hunt the roe and sika deer that tigers need to survive. Tigers need vast, healthy forests. If we protect the forests for tigers, we also protect lynx, black storks and blooming hillsides of rhododendron that are found in the home that they share.

The otters were having so much fun that I wished for a fur coat that repelled water and webbed feet so I could spend my day like them, swimming, bending and twisting in a pool. The otters were at ease in the water, playing with each other, tumbling in the grass and always on the move.

Spotted-necked otters from Africa need large lakes and rivers with clear water and rocky bottoms. If people cut down trees and grow crops on the river banks, soil blows off the land and makes the water cloudy and unhealthy for otters. If we protect the land near rivers and streams and keep the water clean for otters, we also protect the many forest and grassland animals that are found in the home that they share.

The gorillas were busy eating breakfast, sitting high in the branches in their family group. One gorilla left its high tree and padded over to a rocky river bank. It was so close that I could see its fingers and toes. They looked like my own fingers and toes, only much bigger.

Mountain and lowland gorillas are found in Africa. Both species are endangered, which means very few are left in the wild. Gorillas are closely related to humans, and the same diseases we catch can make them sick. Wars in Africa also threaten gorillas and make it hard for people to study and protect them. These animals need humid rainforests and hard-to-reach mountain slopes. If we protect the forests for gorillas, we also protect leopards, black-and-white colobus monkeys, shy okapi and wonderfully odd pangolins that are found in the home that they share.

I walked into a bright blue tunnel of water and stared up as a polar bear swam right over my head! I saw its black padded feet as the bear pushed off the glass ceiling swimming from one glimmering, sun-lit pool to the other. The seals swam back and forth over my head too. I couldn't believe how close I was, watching their eyes, ears, spots, fur and whiskers as they swam above me.

Polar bears are top predators. In their cold, icy world, a polar bear has its babies inside a snowy den. Baby bears are born during the deepest of winter, while the mother is fast asleep hibernating. Polar bears are excellent swimmers, as comfortable in the water as they are on land. Their white fur helps them sneak up on animals when they hunt and also helps keep them from overheating in the warm summer months. Our changing climate is melting the icy world that polar bears and other Arctic animals need to survive. If we protect the Arctic for polar bears, we also protect snowy owls, Arctic fox, walrus, ringed seals, caribou and narwhal whales that are found in the home that they share.

I watched the elephants and imagined that I had a trunk just like them. I would use my trunk to clean my room, splash mud outside and give myself a shower on hot days.

African elephants are the largest of all living land mammals. A baby elephant has to learn how to use its trunk to pick up sticks and spray water much like we have to learn how to hold a pencil and write our name. As elephants move across the landscape, they change the habitat and maintain the grasslands. If we protect African elephants, we also protect rhinoceros, hyenas, cheetahs, lions, wildebeest, zebras and baobab trees that are found in the home that they share.

When I looked into the trees in the panda bear enclosure, I could see only leaves, rocks and flowers at first. Then a patch of black and white flickered through the trees, and the female panda, who will be having her baby soon, sat down in front of me, munching on a stick of bamboo.

Giant pandas live in remote forests of southwestern China. There are about 1,600 pandas living in the wild, and these animals continue to lose the precious forests they need to survive. Zoos support captive breeding programs to help the struggling wild populations. These programs also help us learn how to better protect pandas and their young in the wild. If we protect habitat for giant pandas, we also protect takins, black-necked cranes, red pandas and bamboo forests that are found in the home that they share.

glue in this circle
mount penny here

A lazy day in the bright sunshine seemed to be all the sea lions needed to be happy. As I leaned forward to watch two sea lions, their young pup swam into sight, twirling with ease and grace in a water ballet.

Did you know that you can tell the difference between sea lions and seals because sea lions have little ears that you can see and because they walk quite well on their front flippers? Sea lions make their home both on the land and in the water, so they are affected by changes we make to the land and oceans. When we take too many fish from the oceans and damage the ocean floor, sea lions suffer. Sea lions are also important food for great white sharks and orcas. If we protect sea lions, we also protect the humpbacked whales, squid, crabs, sea otters and the fragile home that they share.

When I looked into the grassy space, at first all I could see was a tangle of tails and ear tips. Then I spotted a pocket, and out popped a baby kangaroo, also called a joey. Kangaroos like to spend hot afternoons sleeping in shady places, but the joeys are always ready to play.

Kangaroos' unique bodies allow them to cross long distances in search of food and water in their Australian home. Kangaroo legs are excellent for jumping. They travel long distances with their big feet and strong tails, hopping even easier than they can run. When kangaroos cross large distances today, they have trouble on roads and often are hit by cars. Many other Australian creatures also find the roads dangerous places. If we protect habitat for kangaroos, we also protect spiny echidnas, duck-billed platypus, wombats, cackling kookaburras and giant cassowaries that are found in the home that they share.

I saw so many animals at the zoo today with my family. If I help take care of these animals and support people working to preserve wild places, our world will continue to be a diverse place full of mammals, birds, reptiles, insects and plants. By preserving habitats of these wild creatures, we also protect our own future. A world with healthy wild places can filter our drinking water, provide our food, keep our climate comfortable and continue to be a home that we all can share.

We saw families in every possible configuration at zoos around the country, getting faces painted, gazing with awe-inspired faces and having fun together watching magnificent animals.

The zoos that inspired the pages you see in *Homes That They Share* are:

PHILADELPHIA ZOO, PHILADELPHIA, PENNSYLVANIA
MINNESOTA ZOO, APPLE VALLEY, MINNESOTA
CHAPULTEPEC ZOO, MEXICO CITY, MEXICO *FREE ADMISSION
OKLAHOMA CITY ZOO, OKLAHOMA CITY, OKLAHOMA
HENRY VILAS ZOO, MADISON, WISCONSIN *FREE ADMISSION
COMO PARK ZOO AND CONSERVATORY, SAINT PAUL, MINNESOTA *FREE ADMISSION
REID PARK ZOO, TUCSON, ARIZONA
LINCOLN PARK ZOO, CHICAGO, ILLINOIS *FREE ADMISSION
DETROIT ZOO, DETROIT, MICHIGAN
SMITHSONIAN NATIONAL ZOOLOGICAL PARK, WASHINGTON, D.C. *FREE ADMISSION
BRONX ZOO, BRONX, NEW YORK
SAINT LOUIS ZOO, SAINT LOUIS, MISSOURI *FREE ADMISSION

This book originated out of our concern for wild places in the world and recognition of the important role zoos have in educating youth and families about conservation. To create this book, we traveled to a dozen zoos in North America to photograph people interacting with animals in exhibits. Nancy took this wide array of photographs, using her artistic skills, and created the illustrations you see in these pages. Any resemblance between specific individuals and the images in this book is purely coincidental. Although only some of the marvelous zoos available to visit are represented here, the species featured are available to be visited in many of the hundreds of zoos in North America. We hope that our efforts inspire you to spend more time looking at the animals, sharing ideas with your children and talking about the animals that make our world so intricate, varied and truly remarkable.

Ten percent of all income Leatherwood Publishing generates from sales of this book is donated to the takhi living in Khustain National Park, Mongolia, to help ensure that they continue to run free in their wilderness home.